American Symbols

The Great Seal of the United States

by Terri DeGezelle

Consultant:
Charlene Bangs Bickford
Director of the First Federal Congress Project
The George Washington University
Washington, D.C.

Capstone press

Mankato, Minnesota

First Facts is published by Capstone Press
151 Good Counsel Drive, P.O. Box 669, Mankato, Minnesota 56002
www.capstonepress.com

Library of Congress Cataloging-in-Publication Data
DeGezelle, Terri, 1955–
     The Great Seal of the United States / by Terri DeGezelle.
     p. cm. —(American symbols)
     Summary: Describes the Great Seal, designed by members of the First Continental
Congress as a symbol of the new nation.
     Includes bibliographical references and index.
     ISBN 0-7368-2528-2 (hardcover)
     1. United States—Seal—Juvenile literature. [1. United States—Seal. 2. Emblems,
National. 3. Signs and symbols.] I. Title. II. Series: American symbols (Mankato, Minn.)
CD5610.D36 2004
929.9—dc21   2003010802

Editorial Credits
Amanda Doering, editor; Linda Clavel, series designer; Molly Nei, book designer and
     illustrator; Kelly Garvin and Scott Thoms, photo researchers; Eric Kudalis and
     Karen Risch, product planning editors

Photo Credits
Capstone Press/Gary Sundermeyer, 5
Corbis/Bettmann, cover, 8, 12, 17, 18, 19
Department of the Treasury, 15
Folio Inc./Anderson, 13; Maroon, 7
Getty Images/Hulton Archive, 9
Library of Congress, 20
North Wind Picture Archives, 11

1 2 3 4 5 6 09 08 07 06 05 04

Table of Contents

Great Seal Fast Facts

★ The Great Seal is stored in the Exhibit Hall of the Department of State building in Washington, D.C.

★ The Great Seal is placed on important papers after the president signs them.

★ Fourteen men helped design the Great Seal. Congress first asked Benjamin Franklin, John Adams, and Thomas Jefferson to design the seal. Congress finally accepted Charles Thomson's design.

★ The Great Seal is on the back of the one-dollar bill.

★ The Great Seal has two sides.

★ The bald eagle on the front of the seal is the national bird, which stands for freedom.

★ The 13 stars and 13 stripes on the Great Seal stand for the first 13 states.

Symbol of a New Nation

In 1782, the Great **Seal** became a **symbol** of a new nation. Since then, the seal has been used to mark important papers. Many images make up the Great Seal. These images stand for beliefs like freedom and peace. The United States was **founded** on these beliefs.

Fun Fact:
A die is a tool that makes the imprint of the Great Seal on paper. Seven dies of the Great Seal have been made.

AND WHEREAS the Senate of the United States of America by their resolution of July 21, 1949, two-thirds of the Senators present concurring therein, did advise and consent to the ratification of the said Treaty;

NOW, THEREFORE, be it known that I, Harry S. Truman, President of the United States of America, having seen and considered the said North Atlantic Treaty, do hereby, in pursuance of the aforesaid advice and consent of the Senate of the United States of America, ratify and confirm the said Treaty and every article and clause thereof.

IN TESTIMONY WHEREOF, I have caused the Seal of the United States of America to be hereunto affixed.

DONE at the city of Washington this twenty-fifth day of July in the year of our Lord one thousand nine hundred forty-nine and of the Independence of the United States of America the one hundred seventy-fourth.

Harry Truman

By the President:

Dean Acheson
Secretary of State

In witness whereof, the undersigned Plenipotentiaries have signed this Treaty.

Done at Washington, the fourth day of April, 1949.

En foi de quoi, les Plénipotentiaires ci-dessous désignés ont signé le présent Traité.

Fait à Washington le quatrième avril 1949.

FOR THE KINGDOM OF BELGIUM:
POUR LE ROYAUME DE BELGIQUE:

P. H. Spaak

Silvercruys

FOR CANADA:
POUR LE CANADA:

Lester B. Pearson

A New Nation

In 1776, the 13 American colonies **declared** their freedom from Great Britain. Men from each colony met in Pennsylvania. They formed a new nation.

Thomas Jefferson's rejected designs

The new nation needed a symbol.
From 1776 to 1781, **Congress** asked
many people to help design the seal.
But Congress rejected all of their ideas.

Congress Approves

In 1782, Congress asked Charles Thomson to design the seal. Thomson used parts of the rejected ideas in his design. On June 20, 1782, Congress **approved** Thomson's design. The United States finally had a seal to **represent** the country. They called it the Great Seal.

Q **Fun Fact:**
Congress took six years to approve the Great Seal.

The Front of the Great Seal

The bald eagle represents freedom. The olive branch stands for peace. The arrows show that the United States will fight for its freedom.

The U.S. **motto** on the ribbon is written in Latin. It means, "Out of many, one." One country was made from 13 states. Thirteen stars stand for each state.

The Back of the Great Seal

The pyramid represents America's strength. The eye above the pyramid represents God. The words on the seal are in Latin. The top words mean, "He favors our undertakings." The bottom words mean, "New order of the ages."

Fun Fact:
The letters carved into the pyramid stand for the date 1776. In 1776, the American colonies declared themselves free from Great Britain.

The Great Seal Today

Today, the Great Seal die is kept in the Department of State building in Washington, D.C. The seal is put on important papers.

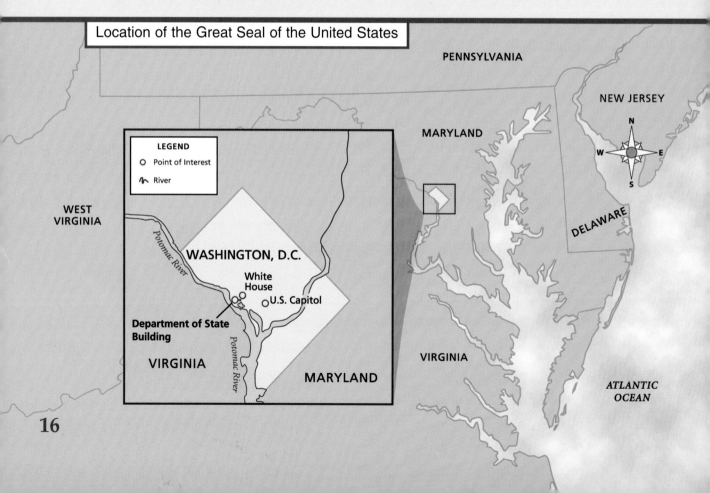

Location of the Great Seal of the United States

PENNSYLVANIA

NEW JERSEY

MARYLAND

WEST VIRGINIA

DELAWARE

LEGEND
O Point of Interest
∿ River

Potomac River

WASHINGTON, D.C.

White House

O U.S. Capitol

Department of State Building

Potomac River

VIRGINIA

MARYLAND

VIRGINIA

ATLANTIC OCEAN

N
W E
S

The Great Seal is still a symbol of the
United States. The seal reminds people
of freedom and peace.

Time Line

June 13, 1782—Congress asks Charles Thomson to design the seal.

July 4, 1776—The American colonies declare independence from Great Britain. Congress asks Benjamin Franklin, John Adams, and Thomas Jefferson to design a seal for the new nation. Their designs are rejected by Congress.

June 20, 1782—Congress approves Charles Thomson's design.

June 26, 1935—The one-dollar bill is approved by President Franklin Roosevelt. The Great Seal appears on the back of the dollar.

1961—The Great Seal is placed in the Exhibit Hall of the Department of State.

1982—The 200th anniversary of the Great Seal is celebrated.

Amazing But True!

On the Great Seal, the eagle's head faces toward the olive branch. This means that the United States is a peaceful nation. But from 1877 to 1945, the eagle on the Presidential Seal used by the president faced the arrows. This showed the president's power during war.

Hands On: Finding Patterns

A number pattern was put in the items found in the Great Seal. Try this activity to find out what the pattern is.

What You Need

a picture of the Great Seal
a magnifying glass

What You Do

1. Count the number of stripes on the eagle's chest. How many are there?
2. Count the number of arrows in the eagle's claw.
3. Count the stars above the eagle's head.
4. Count the leaves on the olive branch. Now count the olives on the olive branch. How many are there of each?
5. Count the letters in the motto, *E Pluribus Unum*.

The amount of each item should be the same. What do you think this number stands for?

Glossary

approve (uh-PROOV)—to accept a plan or idea

Congress (KONG-griss)—the branch of the U.S. government that makes laws

declare (di-KLAIR)—to say something

found (FOUND)—to set up or start something

motto (MOT-oh)—a short sentence that tells what someone believes in or stands for

represent (rep-ri-ZENT)—to stand for something

seal (SEEL)—a design pressed into an important paper or envelope

symbol (SIM-buhl)—an object that stands for something else

Read More

Banting, Erinn. *Flags and Seals.* Mankato, Minn.: Weigl Publishers, 2003.

Yanuck, Debbie L. *The Bald Eagle.* American Symbols. Mankato, Minn.: Capstone Press, 2003.

Internet Sites

FactHound offers a safe, fun way to find Internet sites related to this book. All of the sites on FactHound have been researched by our staff.

Here's how:
1. Visit *www.facthound.com*
2. Type in this special code **0736825282** for age-appropriate sites. Or enter a search word related to this book for a more general search.
3. Click on the **Fetch It** button.

FactHound will fetch the best sites for you!

Index